HEART FIRST INTO THIS RUIN

PRAISE FOR *WICKED ENCHANTMENT*
Edited & Introduced by Terrance Hayes

....

One of the Year's Best Books of Poetry:
New York Times, Washington Post, Irish Times

Winner of the California Independent Booksellers Alliance's
2020 Golden Poppy Award for Poetry

....

"Wildly fun and inventive...and frequently hilarious; they
seem to cover every human experience and emotion."
NEW YORK TIMES

"Required Reading"
BUSTLE

"One of the most exciting, original, deliciously dangerous
voices of the twentieth century."
IRISH TIMES

"A big bold no-holds-barred American voice."
ARTS FUSE

"An essential retrospective."
LIT REACTOR

"Coleman pulls the reader in with long, sinuous lines that
keep driving forward, pulling you along."
HYPERALLERGIC

"Her work pushes us to confront injustice with as much
candor as she did—and with as much care."
POETRY

ALSO BY WANDA COLEMAN

Mad Dog Black Lady (1979)

Imagoes (1983)

Heavy Daughter Blues: Poems & Stories 1968–1986 (1987)

A War of Eyes and Other Stories (1988)

African Sleeping Sickness: Stories & Poems (1990)

Hand Dance (1993)

American Sonnets (1994)

Native in a Strange Land: Trials & Tremors (1996)

Bathwater Wine (1998)

Mambo Hips and Make Believe: A Novel (1999)

Mercurochrome (2001)

Ostinato Vamps (2003)

Wanda Coleman: Greatest Hits, 1966–2003 (2004)

The Riot Inside Me: More Trials & Tremors (2005)

Jazz and Twelve O'Clock Tales (2008)

The World Falls Away (2011)

The Love Project: A Marriage Made in Poetry (2014)

Wicked Enchantment: Selected Poems (2020)

HEART FIRST INTO THIS RUIN
THE COMPLETE AMERICAN SONNETS

WANDA COLEMAN
INTRODUCTION BY MAHOGANY L. BROWNE

BOSTON
BLACK SPARROW PRESS
2022

Published in 2022 by BLACK SPARROW PRESS

GODINE
Boston, Massachusetts
www.godine.com

LIBRARY OF CONGRESS CATALOGING-IN-PUBLICATION DATA
Names: Coleman, Wanda, author. | Browne, Mahogany L., writer of introduction.
Title: Heart first into this ruin : the complete American sonnets /
    Wanda Coleman ; introduced by Mahogany L. Browne.
Description: Boston : Black Sparrow Press, 2022.
Identifiers: LCCN 2021052622 (print) | LCCN 2021052623 (ebook)
    ISBN 9781574232530 (paperback) | ISBN 9781574232547 (ebook)
Subjects: LCGFT: Poetry.
Classification: LCC PS3553.O47447 H39 2022 (print)
    LCC PS3553.O47447 (ebook) | DDC 811/.54--dc23
LC record available at https://lccn.loc.gov/2021052622
LC ebook record available at https://lccn.loc.gov/2021052623

Cover Design Tammy Ackerman
Cover Art Ken Price, West L.A., 1990. Ink on vellum,
6¼ x 10½ inches, 16 x 27 cm. *Copyright* © Estate of Ken Price,
Courtesy Matthew Marks Gallery

First Printing, 2022
Printed in the United States of America

CONTENTS

THIS IS THE CITY WE'VE COME TO

An Introduction

P LUM NELLY WAS a dirt-licked neighborhood in Los
Angeles County. Full of dairy farms, ranches with
horses, and the repelling whiff of cattle. Southeast is
Compton. Far east is El Segunda. Plum Nelly is where my
mother was born to the stench of dirt, cows, sweat, and
blood. "I don't remember much—but I'll never forget the
smell," she says.

"How far is it from Watts?" I ask.

"Well, Watts is all city," she laughs.

When we hang up the phone, I investigate the route
from Plum Nelly, a neighborhood known for teetering
on the county line, right below Inglewood and just seven
miles from Watts.

Watts produced some of the most awakening mo-
ments in our humanity. It housed the rage of the Watts
Uprising, it hosts one of the highest poverty rates in
California, and it produced the brilliant art of Wanda
Coleman.

Wanda Coleman, author of twenty books of poems, unofficially L.A.'s poet laureate and queen of the American sonnet, is researchable. Her attributions and work reverberate, even if you've never heard her read a poem. You can hear her defiant tone in a Robert Glasper jazz note. You can feel her fiery honesty in the lyrics of Melanie Charles. Wanda is everywhere. But it wasn't always this way.

I could talk about her timbre, or her single-parent journey, or her ability to love and lust with the page as open as any warm home. I could write about how her anger fueled the poems, how the sonnet became a container, a structure she could bend to her liking. A tradition to twist back, a reflection of ourselves bare, as the reader reckons with the literary world's distorted reflection.

I could talk about how Wanda suffered no fools. I know that because I studied her work. Terrance Hayes, poet, professor, and Wanda Coleman fan, once wrote, "She denounced boredom, cowardice, the status quo." And this is a fact. She had zero cares for who was offended by her critique because she was thinking critically about how we live and die. She was writing critically about the degradation of Black women, the separation of Black women from white women, as when we first notice who believe they deserve to be saved in the event of an emergency— except the sinking ship is this country, and Black women have never been considered (see "American Sonnet 11").

Wanda was thinking critically about how we move from here when she wrote in "American Sonnet 13":

i already feel my soul's freedom hymns
(*i am drunk on disturbing things, hopelessness flows*
from the wounds of my negritude, when light reaches me
i cringe and pray for darkness to return)

The devil you know, right? The suffering you know, right? Wanda didn't cower to the insistence of doubt: in the face of it, she made certain it knew her name. *Heart First into This Ruin* is a collection of one hundred sonnets placed in numerical order, so the reader can follow Wanda's gentle insistence of discovery and her jagged instructions; our voices would be ravaged clean should we ever find ourselves reading the poems aloud.

Brooklyn isn't Watts. But I live here and walk and order coffee from expensive roasters, and the energy in Crown Heights tells me there is a distinctive relation to Cali. On the corner, a Black woman yells, mouth sky up, and asks, "What am I supposed to do?" to no one in particular. I want to tell her, *Wanda told us what to do.* Instead, I turn to my phone, where friends and I celebrate Wanda's earth birthday with pictures and our favorite lines from her poems. I text her mentee, the author and actress Amber Tamblyn. Because I never met Wanda in real life but was instead raised by her directness (Black women from California quilt and gift the community coordinates of survival for generations to come), I believe it is an offering from the universe to be able to tap in with someone who knew her best. I asked Amber to

talk about Wanda, who was incredibly diligent to the work, despite being labeled "mean."

She responds generously: "Wanda didn't believe in writer's block. She believed we must honor the muse inside us when she is quiet. Wanda could draw blood by crafting a poem with the sharp edges of emotion, she was singular—a voice for the ages and untouchable in her verse."

WHAT IS A sonnet besides fourteen lines written in iambic pentameter?

What is an American Sonnet besides fourteen lines, looser in its musicality and inventive in its ability to transform the tradition into a handheld microphone, a makeshift podium, or the people's anthem?

O Wanda, devout rule breaker, considerate heart mender, your Black woman bravado be spilling everywhere, I sing. A cup of coffee near this keyboard, empty and ringing like a tomb.

O Wanda. Iconic afro. Beauty untethered. The ability to language a freight train back onto its tracks. The ability to erect the building in our chests toward the cloud. It is falling, you know: the sky. What we know to be true—what we've been taught and what've begun to unlearn. All of it is falling. *Heart First into This Ruin: The Complete American Sonnets* is here to breach the gates of complacency.

"To know I must survive myself," she writes in "American Sonnet 7." *To know I must survive myself*, she ends the poem,

with the recognition of our perilous state. We are ticking, these bombs of mass intrusion. This American-conditioning designed to sleep-drunk us silly. We must interrogate the casual racism, the degradation of the Black body, the heat of want, and the power of desire as a mercy. We must interrogate our relationship to power structures, our proximity to privilege, and the way in which we spill tea for fodder, rather than constructive criticism.

Wanda is with us; these poems are the inquiry and the results. Wanda is with us; we are consolidating each atrocity, landmarked for the homies, and allies, and accomplices, and comrades, and sugared lips, and canisters upturned, and our children's laughter as proof: We are still here. Wanda is still here. These poems are proof. The poems she wrote are the gift. The voice she gave us the gift.

In "American Sonnet 6," Wanda asks, "What does fame do without money?" She is asking the reader, the academy, the purveyors of poverty, and those who benefit from Black art without experiencing the trauma, joy, and love that created it: *If I am saving you, with this art and those standing ovations, why can I not afford safe and clean housing? If you can speak my name and tears fall from your face, as if you are in church, as if you have been found, why can I not afford proper health care? Why do my children have to step over potholes so big they're stuffed with garbage cans as they walk to school? Why do the schools in my neighborhoods have metal detectors? Why is the White House not on fire?*

. . .

I AM WAXING poetic, as poets tend to do when faced with their own mortality. Forgive me. Turn to one of my favorite poems in this book, "American Sonnet 4," which begins "Rejection can kill you." Years before I understood my duty as poet/observer, poet/archivist, poet/advocate, and Black woman poet, I knew there was no utopia for my kind. I knew my afro and pout would be too much for some to hold gently. It took me time, but I learned what Wanda lived. Like a true West Coast soothsayer, she only had the know-how to tell it like it is: "This is the city we've come to / all the lights are red all the poets are dead and there / are no norths."

There are no norths. There ain't no norths to run toward. This is it, people. Wanda tried to prepare us: We are the freedom we've been searching for.

—Mahogany L. Browne
Brooklyn, 2021

HEART FIRST INTO THIS RUIN

AMERICAN SONNET

the lurid confessions of an ex-cake junky: "i blew it
all. blimped. i was really stupid. i waited
until i was forty to get hooked on white flour
and powdered sugar"

$$\frac{\text{white greed}}{\text{socio-eco dominance}} \times \frac{\text{black anger}}{\text{socio-eco disparity}} =$$

a) increased racial tension/polarization
b) increased criminal activity
c) sporadic eruptions manifest as mass killings
d) collapses of longstanding social institutions
e) the niggerization of the middle class

the blow to his head cracks his skull
he bleeds eighth notes & treble clefs

(sometimes i feel like i'm almost going)

to Chicago, baby do you want to go?

AMERICAN SONNET 2

for Robert Mezey

for outshining the halos of heaven's greedy archangels
the sensitive nightfall with her dazzling teeth
is sentenced to the eclipse of eternal corporate limbo
the exquisite isolation of endless neon-lit hallways

for the miscegenation of her spirit to earth's blood
for giving her moonrises to tropical desires
powerful executives syphon off her magic
to face the consequences of devilish exploitation

towards the cruel attentions of violent opiates
as towards the fatal fickleness of artistic rain
towards the locusts of social impotence itself

i see myself thrown heart first into this ruin

not for any crime
but being

AMERICAN SONNET 3

fair splay/pay—the stuff myths are made of
(cum grano salis)

that thoughts become things
words weapons

who gives the african violet the right to bloom
rain the right to be wet
who permits the moon to draw menses

i protest this tyranny of ghosts
who reign in the world of letters
would-be-betters

in actuality

pseudo-intellectuals with suck-holes for brains
so dense even when the light goes on
they're still in the dark

today i protest the color of the sky
that is not the color of my skin

AMERICAN SONNET 4

rejection can kill you

it can force you to park outside neon-lit
liquor stores and finger the steel of
your contemplation, it can even make you
rob yourself

(when does the veteran of one war fail to
appreciate the vet of another?)

the ragged scarecrow lusts in the midst of
a fallow field

and the lover who prances in circles envies me
my moves/has designs on my gizzard/kicks shit

this is the city we've come to
all the lights are red all the poets are dead
and there are no norths

AMERICAN SONNET 5

rusted busted and dusted

the spurious chain of plebian events
(aintjahmamaauntjemimaondapancakebox?)

which allows who to claim the largest number of homicides
the largest number of deaths by cancer the largest
number of institutionalized men the largest number of
single female heads of household the largest number of
crimes of possession the largest number of functionally
insane the largest number of consumers of dark rum

largely
preoccupied with perfecting plans of escape

see you later alligator
after while crocodile
after supper muthafucka

AMERICAN SONNET 6

portfolio profligates of creative capitalism
proliferate—wage slave labor intensive

pack up all your cares and dough
here we go interest's low
bye-bye bankbook

pro rata (whacked-out on assonance
and alliteration)

middle management mendacity
(let jesus do it on his lunch hour)

i hit forty before i got my first credit card

zed-to-zed/the game of bird association

when one's only credentials are the holes
in one's tired bend-overs

what does fame do without money?

AMERICAN SONNET 7

to take the outer skin in. rehumanize it

is

swallowing whole the dourness of
an unremitting scorn and unstoppable cruelty
the exploitive ambition of pricey looks
stealing meat off the bone

is

to know grief my unnaming tongue
it reaches for its lyric the mother of
all pain to birth to know this ugly/an
abandoned stillborn blued around its eyes and
bodily bruised. found buried in a dumpster
beneath the rages of an unsung life

is

to know i must survive myself

AMERICAN SONNET 8

not just another marketeer

a billion a year racket owned by
everyday business folk
an exciting all-cash opportunity
the latest schemology! no monthly over head!
run it at home or out of the trunk of your car
can be operated part-time earning you deep
pockets while you keep your regular job
no experience or special training needed
start today with low initial investment

quick returns/the coins stack up
your latest crack at securing a future

try it yourself, it's high-octaine for
maintaining cool under pressure

AMERICAN SONNET 9

love people use things

later a possible emergence as
effortless forms of illumination drift
across the screen of the set/swaying bodies
converging/ghosts of divisions
city after city. oh ruthless decay
—these skin disruptions —
the sport of confession for pay
(loose shoes, tight pussy, warm place to shit)
splendid moments when all visions of ghosts/
convergences/bodies swaying adrift
illuminating new behavioral norms
effortless emergence? possibly. later

use people love things

AMERICAN SONNET 10

after Lowell

our mothers rung hell and hardtack from row
    and boll, fenced others'
gardens with bones of lovers, embarking
    from Africa in chains
reluctant pilgrims stolen by Jehovah's light
    planted here the bitter
seed of blight and here eternal torches mark
    the shame of Moloch's mansions
built in slavery's name, our hungered eyes
    do see/refuse the dark
illuminate the blood-soaked steps of each
    historic gain, a yearning
yearning to avenge the raping of the womb
    from which we spring

AMERICAN SONNET II

the moon is livid white, pacifica boils
we are going under
ship afire the sea pools with blood

women and children first

i cannot swim
and i have been refused a mae west

i fight the mob to board a lifeboat
a bronze-haired aryan roughly grabs me by my arm
his eyes a feast of loathing
a tear tattooed beneath his left orb

"i have as much right to live as anyone"
 i demand, he slams me to the deck

"go back to the jungle where you belong"
 he spits, "and stay there"

AMERICAN SONNET 12

after Robert Duncan

my earliest dreams linger/wronged spirits
who will not rest/dusky crows astride
the sweetbriar seek to fly the
orchard's sky. is this the work i loved?
groves of perfect oranges and streets of stars
where the sad eyes of my youth
wander the atomic-age paradise

tasting

the blood of a stark and wounded puberty?
o what years ago? what rapture lost in white
heat of skin/walls that patina my heart's
despair? what fear disturbs my quiet
night's grazing? stampedes my soul?

o memory. i sweat the eternal weight of graves

AMERICAN SONNET 13

after Sergio Macias

today i'm with you braiding hate into a rainbow
picking up trash off the cement banks of the Los Angeles river
human feces litters the corporate dreams downtown
i already feel my soul's freedom hymns
(i am drunk on disturbing things, hopelessness flows
from the wounds of my negritude. when light reaches me
i cringe and pray for darkness to return)
i navigate through the streets, my compass broken
smashed by a hunk of stormy history.
i savor the stench of auto exhaust and unwashed bodies
sweat stinging the unhappy eyes of my region, the
illuminati enforcers mapping my deathwalk toward night

the eagle preens above our bleeding bear

AMERICAN SONNET 14

summersong escape from the coast, a
mile-high up it's bleak and dry, Denver sky giving
back no breath, i'm looted and burned
an aborted discourse on emotional colonialism/my feelings
no longer my own. the cultural carpetbaggers
have stolen my thunder, betrayed, by Zeus!

begging rescue, the loneliness of cool baptismal light
church on a childhood of Sundays—whitest walls
of virgin stucco, oblation —
the seduction of high desert heat

on my knees i drink the wine

my heart assumes the flesh of a two-year-old
thumps like waves rising in my chest
leaps into wonder, drowns

AMERICAN SONNET 15

dear most important believer

on behalf of everyone i'd like to thank you
for your trust and loyalty. to recognize
you as among the sincerest of followers. i'm
pleased to personally welcome you to the many
privileges and benefits. you'll enjoy exclusive
advantages unavailable to others. because you deserve
special attention. i've enclosed your emblems
of guaranteed earned recognition. please take a moment to
contemplate and admire them. we've gone to great lengths
to exceed your every expectation. if you have any questions
about a higher level, remember there is none. if
you feel you need extra recognition this is all there
is since it is special indication of your status

thank you for showing us your best

AMERICAN SONNET 16

after Huey P. Newton

the clairvoyant activist ever ready to
face the consequences of his/her perceptions must

subsist on stubborn hope (D. Brutus) for maintenance
aids dogged determination to construct required change.
revolutionary homicide/suicide means awareness of
reality in combination with potential sociocentrism.
those ill-equipped to struggle against brutal powers risk
extinction. [to cooperate in the imprisoning of one's own
people-psyche is reactionary homicide/suicide which will be
rewarded by ever-watchful scions of the oppressive belief
system. but to pretend to do so is to trick.] specific
group resistance of rampant narco/necromania may be
manifest in periodic eruptions of spontaneous civil
violence. It is imperative that visionaries see

war as ultimate service for resolution

AMERICAN SONNET 17

i am seized with the desire to end

my breath in short spurts, shoulder pain
the world lengthens then contracts
(in deep water—my sudden swimming, the surface
breaks, thoughts leap, the Buick bends
a corner, an arc of light briefly sweeps the dark walls)
everywhere there are temples of stone
and strange chantings—ashes angels and dolls
i forget my lover, i want a stranger—
to shiver at the unfamiliar touch of the one
who has not yet touched me

a furred spider to entrap my hungers
in his silk, with virulent toxin
to numb my throat

AMERICAN SONNET 18

after June Jordan

this is the place where all the lives
are planted in my eyes. black things writhe
on the ground. red things gush from
volcanic gaseous tremblings/become blood and light
mountains of flesh raging toward rapturous seas
where crowns of trees inspired by flame extol the night

(my abysmal heart compels the moon compels
wave upon wave. compels reason)

the tombs are fertile with sacred
rememberings. the ancient rhymes. the
disasters of couplings. the turbulent blaze of
greed's agonies. shadows reaching for time and time
unraveling and undone.

sky river mother—your tongue plunders my mouth

AMERICAN SONNET 19

faster harder
he moans to his imaginary lover

be wary of those who cannot read in bright light
those blinded smiles seem so enchanted so wise so kind
they show what they think they know of feeling yet
know nothing and do not believe that anything at all
can be felt, they rub up against flesh and map its
destiny with the swiftness and certainty of geometry. with
eager fists they translate cries into grammars of pleasure.
nightmares into treatises on desire, nowheres into
comfortable
finalities. their seduction the bookish cat which mauls the
flitting bird, beware the love-starved hands that twitch.
beneath the table's philosophy. fingers like razors dismember
tenderness with mean-minded diatribes, eat every word

AMERICAN SONNET 20

by moonlight the lost is again found
he breaks and enters thru the upstairs window. divests the
dust of its treasures, awakes the ticking of a clock
gone mad. frightens the mirror into confessing

the intruder wields his pistol/invades her praline gloom
candles. incense. the radio's fever—a ballad for
the somber dreamer. black nylon and yellow toile
her voice is thick/dislocated from the beauty of her face

these are all the secrets i have, she shrieks. take them

he lowers the weapon. cautions. will do no harm. offers
his ears. she returns the tears to her eyes
there's no longer a need to call the authorities. his crime
has become an art of faith

AMERICAN SONNET 21

this den of grieving houses the apocryphon
in which he uncovers her/8x11-inch sheets tossed
in languid ritual of coauthorship, fingers claw his
portfolio, bookmark meaning in apian movement of
lines/eyes begging/schizophasia. phallic primacy—his
tongue surrounds her as he lowers his voice, enters
and subjugates her perfumed yet kinky vocabulary

all she utters is his name, repeatedly. then—
earth rumbles then tremors then quakes

she creates a new language of stilted breath/*dzugu*
jukes his ears only, between them coffee stained pages
burned and written and burned again, smoldering
in the aphotic archives of passionate mind

the lover of the poet eats the poet, comes

AMERICAN SONNET 22

" 'twould be better,' said the gypsy, "were you
from another country and not from their coal closet"
no one anoints me. i anoint myself with my own oil
purchased with my mad black lucre earned by the
grace of the blind

spotless hard swept and daily dusted. no visitors.
overhead the ceiling crackles/change riddles the fevered
white plaster/my wakings, vermin infest my politics. i
don't function at the junction anymore, rage rots my
stomach, no resolve, something heavy and skeletal tugs
the boots from my man-sized feet, blue air chills
my feet. strange rings circle my feet

caffeine i cry. *caffeine!* and tear these tumors from
my glory like stones from a quarry

AMERICAN SONNET 23

after Akhmatova

here's to my ruined curbless urban psyche/the spent
tempest fleeing the golden rain of cruel day
wandering star-starved punched-out bleached-blind

here's to the poison i greedily consume as sustenance
to the killer humdrum of my life without fulfillment
my love's isolation, my nation and me—our bickerings

i drink the cold ugly of funky negro divas who
cast me down their death-dealing amused eyes
delighting in my writhing/castration/made numb
in this world—made brutal made coarse made jealous of
they who have usurped and commodified god

here's to

my uncompromising vision and to the young blood who
tells me i carry the broom like a cross

AMERICAN SONNET 24

i'm on uptime/have no resting place/cannot rest
constant strive constant drive
getting into bed is an act of creation. i'm putting
on weight and hope with unequaled relish—trapped twixt
the
illusion of escape and the hallucination of release

i am the love wish of secret rapists/the men
who break before they enter
they fight to maintain the myths i die by
(when underthegun who has time to keep a war journal?)

in that blues pocket of need reed where sweet darkness
begins befogged in the snooze of mist, my legacy
the slave-soaked night wailings of misbegotten dreamers
beseeching the dead to rise once more—that fierce
hoodoo of humans consumed in the defiant flames of living

AMERICAN SONNET 25

today the villains are all named willie
with bushy wild hair which grows heedlessly
spewing discontent/a new breed
of resilient superlice disrespecting all borders
and infesting the puritan scalps
of bloody-handed dealers in cyclopean confusion

each death carried in blank eyes
(they taught us to accept the strangeness
of tolerance) someone discovers a mind
missing for over a decade
making note that all phone messages are from
neglected dunners irate over negligence

this compulsion to write one's name
is a form of post-recession autoeroticism

as we undergo national ustulation

AMERICAN SONNET 26

for and after Michelle T. Clinton

kicks & jams & slams

too nice too sincere too there. but lovemonger—
without you this city is a pale rude fiction. your
womanly radiance kept the all-knowing crowing. so
no way can i forget you though jealous dark hides you
cloaks you in a sentimental shape-changer's sufferings. i
will not forget. you. sweetsistuh goodheart
candle-burner/flame-keeper. *gimme sommadat toast.*
(my blood pressure runs low. deep hypotension)

ooohgo if you must. blow that escape hatch—rubyfruit

flee this sham world. yessum. your leavings a
dreamtrail of sweet snickerings
along this parched desert floor where deviltongues
ache for the magic rush of your angelgush

AMERICAN SONNET 27

after F. A. Nettelbeck

who i wasn't was that kink-wig stereotype tossed bills
        for nibble—blatant motive of aged honky boozer
who sprouted pages and flew when The Muse spread those
        thorny androgynous gams under his gross flabby
gut imbuing his colossal coarseness with exquisite seizure

        o

'twasn't on the tab, nevertheless i was meted distance
        at a smile indisputably for my good, who i was was
twice witness when that besotted Saint of The Downtrodden
        loosed belt, dropped trousers and displayed the ugliest
purplest most revolting truths in the history of the pulp, so

        here's to the spook of unwashed urinals and skidrow
hells! may the beerpiss prose of his glory ever grace
        overripe whores going down without nipping, his legacy
the art of keeping toilet paper from sticking to fingers

AMERICAN SONNET 28

how much juice rutabagas givin' up these days?
beans, feverish hardworker/rut-intensive of simple
poverty-struck tastes i've never had much/reward
relative to my statistical status
(if rich by standards of starving mobs).

last night, over dry blond bubbly, we toasted
having both—money and man—that gypsy and i. she
said nail-it-to-the-cross before sixty, otherwise
you're courting bitter withered cronehood
(like her *baleboosteh behayma babushka* who spent
knees and sanity polishing corporate marble to
keep ten crumbcatchers and her *momzer).*

whoa, gottaget with savvy politic and long-term whoopy
otherwise, the tarot forecasts panic weather

a black spasm on a brokedown bed

AMERICAN SONNET 29

after Wolfgang Hildesheimer

it does not fly. ideological plumage/a white
withered boa—signature of ancient flappage
stunted economic growth, grounded/
skyless, flirtings at air

i have three wings, with whom do i flock?

the gypsy gives me a silver coin
tells me to pouch it in leather tells me
love is its own context

(he found the check in the mailbox before i
got home, cashed it and spent it on vein feed)

transforming myself into night, i fall/shadows
across troubled days—memories mirrored in 5
empty ron rico bottles/brew for minor bitchlips

parched and chirping for his
"you look like money" kiss

AMERICAN SONNET 30

after Chris Gilbert

getting into me this year/i'm wasted/am ever to
be an infernal blackwoman in which zip time is
properly mine, never fashionable, from breath
to death it's all skin trouble and misreadings.

ladadedadedadaada — splaaapblaap

a joke. oooh. hard expectorations — headwinds rushing
and then keeping love satisfied and at bay. the
price extracted for a tight space in some late
pepsi generation who's where, *taxed maxed waxed*

subsequendy the siren becomes a witchywoman, her
gnarled arms branches clawing sky for transformative
angelsongs/soulnotes to seed deepblooming roses in
the bigotheart — the art? survivor pulled from
flames i curse rescue, cry "letttt me burn"

AMERICAN SONNET 31

now bongos play remorse (verse of course)

requiem for comrade boheme betrayed whose
remains will never be aired—not on radio or TV.
a nouveau silent movie? perhaps not—the debate
a liar's feast ending in outlaw's tears and
gun-riddled pleadings for embrace/sugarsweet scent
of slow-rotting visionary denied more days

justice speaks your name rude friend your name
murderer your criminal shame mere bones of dreams
polished clean by producer and consumer/cannibalized
have no grave—exiled to Apennine ruins

rend open this death-row cell that i may flee

lo! the bard's winged hands transcendent
split this earth. ancient drums new beats

AMERICAN SONNET 32

for Bliss Carnochan

there are few ways i know of by which i can
escape being symbolic, self-dramatization of my
random victimization has proven skunk in a zoo
of Siamese cats, but once having undergone ethno
scramblization am i doomed to be just another
pathogoggler conforming to the dominant mode?
                                            just
another deviant excluded from the conversation?

in this universe a power restrains me. fear
and waste abound, in the pathological pursuit
of his beauty, my truth is mortified

o fortune's wind, when wilt thou blow
        that the large coin down can rain?
kkkrist, that money were in my palms
        and i in my wits again

AMERICAN SONNET 33

hams & jams damn gams of ma'ams
fuels an industry of diet scams

fat gathers like bad weather/forecasts
a malfunctioning heart, those bums of thunder
he loves to plunder so deeply in the dark
now spread too widely under the stresses of an
endless quest for excellence and art—reveal
frustrations expressed in overtly oral
administrations of treasures à la carte, o
grease o chocolate o salt o permutations from
grapevine—dullings of disappointment's edge
explode the wasteline, trapped in mirror's
mud a slimmer glimmer dwells/a starker
sweeter dish flambéed intensely if not well

AMERICAN SONNET 34

after Jones/Baraka

call me a rebel angel
firstborn & full-time resident of lower hell

my eyeballs are shot thru with the heavy crimson
blood of an honest race. my skin is musky dusky—
wings shriveled useless lacquered to my back by
generations of theopathy (o perverse astasia). i be

large-lipped prodigal oracle nappy assignations
the long shadow of my psychosexual dehumanization
blotting out all suns. i rule agony's pit

Dis messenger! i have heard you blow
treble treble roil and revel
and would rise to dance in the millennium. but

my feet fail me. now. so edematous
i can't force them into my Tiffany slippers

AMERICAN SONNET 35

boooooooo. spooky ripplings of icy waves, this
umpteenth time she returns—this invisible woman
long on haunting short on ectoplasm

"you're a good man, sistuh," a lover sighed solongago.
"keep your oil slick and your motor running."

wretched stained mirrors within mirrors of
fractured webbings like nests of manic spiders
reflect her ruined mien (rue wiggles remorse
squiggles woe jiggles bestride her), oozy Manes spill
out yonder spooling in night's lofty hour exudes
her gloom and spew in rankling odor of heady dour

as she strives to retrieve flesh to cloak her bones
again to thrive to keep her poisoned id alive

usta be young usta be gifted—still black

    thin boy no grin boy to eat is a sin boy
self-starved for her sake his mother works so hard to
    feed them curses their births not exactly
but beloved man dad his eternal prison sentence makes
    her burden of fat late night sobbings and
thins the boy his sister his babybrutha o mother—tons
    of heavy lonely a sadmad wageburner's minimum
life all work no fun to feed his sister his babybrutha o
    thin boy *worried love of momomom* so he eats
less and less and less than less to lift their bulk from
    her drudge-spent shoulders-—all he's able
to do a thirteen-year-old so wraithfully thin when he
    turns sideways he vanishes from headlines
deader than economic boom news becomes bones blades
    razor sharp spadings into solid inky soil

AMERICAN SONNET 37

childlove, we're estranged o'er wicked hours

clocked to seed babysitters fatten landlords
the city the country the state the flag, i must
fuel the car and, at smoky intervals, amblers who
press on after stumbles thru, so i won't see
you till late, you'll be asleep, childsonsweet.
i'll be deadwalking my mad slave-driven feet

too bonetired too cashpoor to nurture proper
like says The Law strangling my motherhood
manchild so angry so troubled so never understood

minutes gone to years, dearest flesh, still

our world won't let us hearttime, you won't see
me till later, too late, i'll toss with loss
but do grave sleeping, you—the daunting

AMERICAN SONNET 38

after William Blake

something in here distaff flies

bats and dives and falls and skitters
heart? soul? mind gone foul
my eyes all jitters cannot see what Elohim
imprisons me/has made condemnation of my
sex/has made my skin my people hex

he loves to strum and "steels" my blues
cops my licks and slays my muse
then stretches out my broken wing
and mocks the song i'm pained to sing

Nepenthe offers me no drink
as potent as his hatred's stink
what sport will purchase liberty?

doth he who caged the beast cage me?

AMERICAN SONNET 39

no ZZZs louise, dere's a virusconspirus

blue paisley terror don't want gorgeous moon don't
care about the orange cat gone stray can't worry
about failures to drop a bomb big enough to blast us
out of privation or into major note. can't sweat rent

in arrears, renegade raffia or corner-consuming arachnid
or the sooty blackness clogging airwaves brainwaves
and national arteries. or ghost-eyed latinos begging
work at the backdoor while ebony men beg gang-related
donations for magic bullets at the front. i'm

beset by reams of withering promise belly-up and
spasming on my desktop, immobilized in demonic clockrock,
French-roast flooding the split in my noggin, eyes
rafting walls. foot-to-butt—get it crackin' bitch!
too soon to quit too late to cry

communications/breakhead. i was 'sposed to but
didn't have booktime

bagged, put in a diversity trick: had to know but
once in the know, knowledge didn't break the fall

play or be played, i wanted to be honest with
him. the breakup was a bleeding success

hard to relate to (therefore soft), he is
at his best when being broken into.
negative gyrations about it. mainstreaming to
draw more of them/breakdancing

civilized animosity informs stilted dialogue,
intermission, a change of reels/associations/
batteries—break-in potential

are we large and in charge yet?

AMERICAN SONNET 41

after Philomene Long

every death a haunting/deep sleep of word
lives pass and overlap their cadence a farewell
dreamlessly streaming in slumber in rising
feet glow and drop to the floor/blooms
taking root, becoming limbs, climbing after light

it is unfashionable to rhyme, to adorn sound with
pain, content with manner, to spitefully whisper
in Spenserian ink or Shakespearean blush, it is
passe to slip into paper/wear parchment's timbre
stained saffron and rose with splendor's overflow

    crosslegged, the poet dripping moon
    from spirit torn collects
    the leavings of her pillow
    and pens her book of stone

AMERICAN SONNET 42

uncanny, a gash in the superstructure somewhere
(surely a dream?) fiduciary waters roaring, only
last night the steward was serving pale champagne, i
had none, there was dry ale for my bitter thirst, but
always the possibility of a successful run and
someday and in my own steam—champagne,
calm dread denial shatters with panic's simmer
now all hands stand alert, bailing, pumping, consuming
the brew of sweaty doom, we know as we stoke
we're going under the mighty and the weak alike
we're going down, no horror-relief, no comic rescue,
such slow agony this daily drowning
   some fool has let go of dignity
   giggles uncontrollably

AMERICAN SONNET 43

i am listening for your footfalls, life!
i am here. waiting. with my ancient hammer, a
hangman's rope and a butcher's knife. i shall
pound your head as you ease through the door.
i shall drag your groggy body into the gloom
and dispel it. i shall bind your wrists and
hold you for ransom. i shall steal your laughter
and drink your pain. from your confusion i shall
fashion songs, dance and chant my victory stomp
a ritual my father passed over done taught me

    the lotus moon is a lover's wound
    it frees the red/my bloodjoy
    runs running running
    soaks the earth

AMERICAN SONNET 44

after Stephen Kessler

brewing bathwater for wine she rises from the flaming
tureen of unconsciousness wearing nothing
but native fangs and talons—the welcome rampage of
mouth emitting sighs. so beyond the Irish of
inspiration. so set for arousing tender shrieks for
attention and cravings for ice. alive
with poisonous awareness. every lover perishes with
the memory of her sculpted skin, intuitively absorbed, becomes
flawed masterpiece blasted to fluorescent space junk by her
cacophony of slaughter and the quiet talk of stars

somewhere they are unearthing the evidence
that a heart existed to match the skilled
petrified grace and implacable face buried in a lost
yet scholarly file. desperate for a drop

AMERICAN SONNET 45

for E. Ethelbert Miller

i do deep paper poopoo. rebellious bowels and
righteous stooping give me bragging rights. no
jazz about bluesmen twanging broken heartstrings or
hollow logs or rocks lumping up satin-sheeted beds
or hounddog bloods wailing sweetmamas while working
backwoods chaingangs and strumming up slave-rhyme
in Texarkana jails, no mama don't allow no saxophones
in here, no mama don't dig Harlem vamps or moonlight
slummings with downtown tramps or spinning yarns in
rail-yard camps, no take it mellow my educated fellow, no
reds no blues no po'thang news no hippity-whos. less about

quality, it's still more about
what you suck who they own
what they will or won't politic
how long and how much you swallow

AMERICAN SONNET 46

after Joseph Bathanti

blood-splashed leaves cling to a porous moon-soaked walk
suggest failed escape and ebbing consciousness
emotion-gorged, a trail pocked by steel casings, confused
by the scuffle of inquisitive sneakers and killer shoes—
angellight—and in its beam the winged intruder descends
crimeward, sinking into a night of blades and blackened eyes,
trees genuflect in the wind, witness swift midnight shushings,
the crude wrench of psyche from soma, shelter newborn ghosts,
after a breakfast of headlines, runners jog the neighborhood,
circle the event marked off by yellow tape and moody uniforms,
sightseeing arouses gratitude—some disquiet in
close whispers, prayers from the fearful lucky—deep
in shock-inured souls like blight unsettling the city
once industry fails and a mean prosperity hurries south

AMERICAN SONNET 47

after Ugo Foscolo

my adolescent fatherland is plagued by fear's outbreak
pustules of public mendaciousness erupt like boils on godhead.
i would medicate it—urge maturity—soothe with a balm of tears
and heartbane, but i moan alone in my stinkhole, scribble
insanely the whole telling, how my mind, leveled again and
again, has been rebuilt in splendor over traffic-ridden squalor

and liquor dens, i have been touched by The Sacred and The Bard
yet fail to ease my melancholy soul with psalm, erasing and
rewriting and erasing until all light is extinguished in an
avalanche of paper, beneath the rubble my arthritic clawings

toward what?

the day has arrived when the blind beggar strays through
the plain of smokes, gropes among the dead whose pain is
not assuaged, makes her way into the crypt, takes an urn
to her lips, consumes ash for nourishment

AMERICAN SONNET 48

marginal survivors of abuse by The Savages In Control
suffer chronic delusions of escape following jizzmic
bulimia—ofttimes uttering jabber 'bout colorblind
hebben post-wallow in skintight consumerism

(don't you know they own all the drums now and
have placed the jungle off limits to you? having
become zillionaires by investing
heavily in your cowardly limitations, psychic
dysfunction and boogie rhythms? the baby
you orphaned keeps them in platinum toilets

while ashy rumps sanctimoniously romp sans
concern for either authenticity or Vaseline, still i'm
of you and my will burns to resuscitate the
righteous rage of our split millennialism)

AMERICAN SONNET 49

my cash-starved seducer with blueviolet skin
croons Alabama-tinged bossa nova over tall tan equatorial
lovelies strolling the white sands of bikini-laden
beaches where coconut palms nod sedately
beneath cloud-flecked azure the sun frying
neurons like high-grade hallucinogens
as he simultaneously hugs the mike and my thighs
locking my big browns with his big browns
making salacious promises to lick me into next week

but, jive on ice, we are chained in the brimstone
dungeon of passionate dada (dat sumpthin' wronginus
stronginus), flurried in our copious colloquy
on The Ultimate Answer—greed feeding greed—each
hoping the other knows the sideway up

AMERICAN SONNET 50

the script calls for mock CLOSE UP

accused of homicide, and worse, miscegenation
the all-American ebony hero nods off on camera
lulled by tedious testimony as court resumes

only The Cavalry or MacArthur or Spike can save him
from hard if dubiously profitable time or that
notorious reefer-smoking hanging judge, a former
Lutheran, who rides around town with a dead saxophone
player decomposing in his brains or that pseudobrutha
whose skin condition turned him into Elvis

image remains power, and without air time for sound bites
the vanguard falls quiedy into arrears. FADE TO that
black which is all inclusive, like death
or serious money

of late/too late Our Man Friday discovers
Hollywood was the revolution

AMERICAN SONNET 51

in my last incarnation i inoculated myself
with oodles of dago red and stumbled into fame
without falling. i worshipped in the temple of Lady Day
and took Coltrane as my wizard. i always wore my mink coat
to the Laundromat and drank pale champagne with my

soft-boiled eggs. i believed King Kong got a raw deal.
i believed great and prolonged sex cured cancer. i believed
in the afterdeath. i was liberator of cough-and-gaggers
from the cages of their spew. i scavenged rusted auto parts,
built a niggah machine, loaded it with atomic amour and

wiped out all purveyors of poverty... swapped my pink
pearl for a black sapphire. and then one quincentennial
i rose from the magnificent effluvium of my jazz
to discover my children did not know me

AMERICAN SONNET 52

dearest cousin,

   i am shamed by my own hotheadedness my own
fevered willingness, another mightn't bedevil herself
   so with innuendo and speculation, but i am
indulgent because i know the base nature of ambition so
   well, few miracles are expected in these stark
and dreary quarters, no gallant savant engages my genius
   outside myself, this crude and constant combat
worries and wearies, distraction cloys and confuses, another
   realm would spell relief and release—the beauty of
unfettered discourse, the reverence of a mind's stretch, i pray
   for winelight and salvation in fool's heaven.
i strive to conceal these overwrought self-reproaches from
   malicious eyes, but am consumed by hours of gloom,
doom's language my fatal folly, i am drugged and tormented
   by these betrayals these giddy fingers

AMERICAN SONNET 53

dearest cousin,

upon my sword, it seems i've abandoned the concrete
for the flower, the street for the tower, i feel as
    if i've spent the last five hundred years
picking cotton without pay or shade, my soul remains the
slave and i am shackled to the stone of my inextinguishable
    grief, i rue my own bleeding maw. if only
there were some escape from this dark dreary flesh, in it,
i am denied the beauty of effective discourse, the fruit of
    intellectual ascension, instead, i wallow
in the mundane routine of ceaseless doings, but for my
children, i strive to conceal such anxious and indulgent
    examinations, i suspect i am being consumed
by some mysterious fatigue and fear of the truth drives
me to abstractions, i loathe and curse the terrible
    scribe quilling this loonytoon history

AMERICAN SONNET 54

dearest cousin,

forgive this ruined narrative begging the first
element of creation. last time i was here i was here.
now i wonder what, exactly, are the components of my
invisible spectrum? sun-ra rising.

i went for a reading of palms to rediscover
disappointment. "better an almost-was," said the gypsy,
"than a never-was." her peculiar conjure left me staring at
my naked brown feet for hours. when reverie broke it was
near dawn, mist had occluded the volcano and i found
myself old, alone sans shelter from the ever-blessed heat.

this note is sent perchance you've wondered what
befell one adventuresome one solongago lost, this missive
in an empty ron rico bottle set adrift on a sea of flute
music—this repetitious rendering of pain—for on my
one-palm island dwells no such beast as joy

AMERICAN SONNET 55

after Elinor Wylie

down to the stingy stringy marrow of my mojo rant
there's something in race matters that's atwitch
i loathe the bitchlook, austere immaculate
of deathscapes drawn in pastels and pearly monotones
there's something my lusty afrogenius bemoans
barren holes and cold silver on a sky concrete
a thread of sputum, churned to murky spate
streaming thru slanted gutters culled from stone
i loathe indifferent flags, the blue and the gray
a nation's shelves ill-stocked rendering meager feed
reparation briefer eden than the apple-eater's breath
sullenness, the red-winged descends, alights to stay
swift vengefulness like fire to the reeds
inflames my vigilant soul denies it rest

AMERICAN SONNET 56

coffee bar meditation: "almost human,"
goes the chant, not a judgment but an
observation made prayerfully over sugarless
aromatic caffe Americano grande newly
brewed from fresh ground beans imported
from plantations employing peon labor in a
deeper woollier south, alone between stages
in too tight a space filled with classic
60s riffs (which are ignored by predominantly
younger ears, might as well be pop), and me?
the loftiest of spooks, my haunting insignificant
given the roster of possible frights, i won't
bother, ectoplasm has its price, i'll save these
niggah-flavored boos for heavy waitings ahead

AMERICAN SONNET 57

after Abdul o. Shakur

mid-nightmare, this warning from the slams arrives:

*you have entered the creative sovereignty of an
infamous black postmodernist raptivist who will
not be held accountablefor the rhythms of word
takingyour mind hostage, demandingyour conscience as
ransom, openly defiant and artistically incorrigible, i
define and defend my expression erupting from the bowels
of mainstream conformity, the deathrage in my pen has
overthrown the dictators of mediocrity, my war spirit
transcends the constraints of physical entrapment, they
say that i'm a criminal but my pen is exonerator. i see
what all are blind to, for my eyes are compelled.
i am the rain, the cloud, the thunder, i am that black
tempest of providence inviting you into my soulwind*

AMERICAN SONNET 58

for Susan Anderson

sadness dulls the bliss of my motherings

and sometimes when i feel the first ache of new menses,
weeping for my children blues me over, it's then when
i retrieve cries from cradles out beyond the edge of years
hughughug and realize that somewhere
in this immense complexity of trial and effort

i couldn't feed 'em proper even when i starved
myself, i couldn't draw a man to fill
the void called daddy, i couldn't be daddy.
i couldn't earn a daddy's pay

sometimes the walls shout snot and whisper and
there's tremblings down in my sorry boots, i am
ever the woman with little to offer save
leavings of her manic frothings which, when
dropped to earth, are absorbed without trace

AMERICAN SONNET 59

there proliferates a multitude of warring legends,
tales of false, fabulous and phantasmal character
concerning the abandonment of my natural senses—
i, who am ancient of soul and triply ancient in
travails, i who have grown vertiginous under weighty

knowings, am compelled to record this truth ere it
fade utterly from 20th Century lore—how, in my mean
ekings i have again and again survived calamitous
psychosocial afflictions, extrapunitive and ectogenic

in my counterpose, but of late the specter of
long-suppressed terror has seized my forebrain
causing episodes of somnambulism, dysgnosia
and parorexia, in my quest for cure i'm driven
to self-excision of predatory psi malignancies

burning candles and throwing bones

AMERICAN SONNET 60

white tequila white moon white lies

wyoming love symphony yellowstone afire there's
nothing there but there wyoming wampum our national
treasure the whole damned state is pure park nothing
in wyoming but K-Mart. way out west in the wondrous wilds
of wyoming (i love toby. you mean my husband? no, your
dad) beautiful beauteous wyoming of the waltzing with bear
and jackrabbit run lifers wyoming lotta beer tribesmen
stuck on reservations doomed to sundance on the purple
wyoming sage forever where all the rusted-out chassis go
to die wyoming big blue sky death/dead of quiet peopled
by renegade spirits glass entombed arrowheads where once
was the Shoshone the big whiteness of New Spain and
sun-weathered leathery wyoming hide and shall we gather
at the big wind river and boil it all down to glory

AMERICAN SONNET 61

reaching down into my griot bag
of womanish wisdom and wily
social commentary, i come up with bricks
with which to either reconstruct
the past or deconstruct a head. dolor
robs me of art's coin
as i push, for peanuts, to level walls and
rebuild the ruins of my poetic promise. from
the infinite alphabet of afroblues
intertwinings, i cull apocalyptic visions
(the details and lovers entirely real)
and articulate my voyage beyond that
point where self disappears

mis violentas flores negras
these are my slave songs

AMERICAN SONNET 62

going into a jellyroll, bones threaten
surrender, luck is what you take by force cunning
trickery nerve—mother africa wit.

(when what starts as reward ends as punishment)

who laughs true laughs best, the getaway
the sweetest ride—the theft of thief's booty,
the richest score/quality fat

> "i wannabe able to enjoy this while i've got
> hair 'n my dick's still hard."—Harv

of late, convinced i can turn lead into bread
but am trapped between flesh and spirit
with a throb-on for Johnny Ace and Max Beckmann,
have been blue since the rebirth of
civilization and black for as long as memory.

worry about me

AMERICAN SONNET 63

after Sesshu Foster

cornfields, porker farms, hills rolling down
to the blessed Mississippi, it's ninety percent
white, no good restaurants in town

yearly, drunken college boys drown, pulled under.

football and wrestling are big. nobody takes
literature seriously—stuff by colored folk—it's all
barroom stories and nigger jokes

the young males while away fey times with late-hour
heavy sousing and obscene rhymes, wise young women
dodge competition with males, assemble their
doweries and sharpen their veils

it's so inbred the gene pool's a swamp, elitists and
outsiders don't have much fun. they're afraid of
that *sumpthuri* grown deep in these parts where
chomping on corncobs is one of the arts

AMERICAN SONNET 64

this here majik douse of ice water to awaken a snoring
        magnitude of dissatisfactions
and refusals to do without, the cold will drive to heat.
        a monkey's paw, its sinister hand,
to break any fall, this pistol contains one shot—use it wisely
        like the eyes in the back of
your second head, shed excess weight, take corners cautiously,
        joyjuice is poison, avoid pushers
in gowns and beads, use music to relieve pain, apply desire
        sparingly, here, a strong black
soul and a broken cage door so you don't die a fool with
        your embarrassment on draped
in gold-and-black and smothered in grinning roses while
        some sorry taxed-your-ass sax
ophone poots tasteless last toots about who-don't-know
        but we won't speak ill of

AMERICAN SONNET 65

after Brecht

from blonde shores and languid childhood lulls
the sweep of aquamarine carries weight down
opal and obsidian eyes shine strangely there
as if some golden vision mitigates despair

starlight gleams eternal in the endless smoke
of night while day has been suspended as dawn
and dusk are wed and counting hours has ended once
timelessness begins and who sleeps is woken

arms and more arms cling about the chest until
they slowly draw the sighing from the breasts, cool
fish ring cool thighs on this, the final trip as
laminaria and Irish moss embrace each fingertip

below, the loved downed in somber drift
into God's deep, renowned on every wave as
spume and coastal wind and shadow zone

AMERICAN SONNET 66

after Vallejo

i am dying in lala in a blizzard of sun where
my killers always profit from my death.

look here at the flat little rectangle of embossed
gray stone/the evidence of days. and there, the ants have
taken over speeding busily to and from the oblivious
hill. something tiny yet beautiful has declared
root, an absurd pinkness. and over there, its white
sister. and listen. the precious costly silence broken
only by the distant sigh of an airship's landing and the
aria of a sad bird on its sagging wire above the unkempt
yard. so many's the years one must pay till paying is
up. and only the lucky find their ways underground

oh. thirst. oh. pride.

i am dying in lala in a sunblaze in
a dream dreamt then forsaken

AMERICAN SONNET 67

in this my mean white universe i'm sandwiched between
a lower-case zee and a period, my tongue plays tricks on me.
something roars, in my injurious solitude my legs have deserted
me. morning finds me under attack by the linen, and my
recalcitrant feeties will not get themselves out of bed.

the roar of something unseen moves toward me. i've lapsed
into a strange malaise inhabited by dispersed lives
and jilted grooms-of-christ. an anxious neurotic distorts my
eden with voracious snails, not to mention my bruised backside
sustained when my beloved Adam dropped me onto the concrete.

this unexpected & inescapable clarity breeds
torment, above me now, the demonic roar
of invisible bees, is it mere destiny to
be entangled and stung into stupidity?

AMERICAN SONNET 68

for Tod Machover

my executioner paints kisses on my mirror, that
master peckerwood of death's architecture unveils a
new work of art. i wonder, is my lover bothered by
my absence in some sublime way? or does he
plunge, ironic and deadpan, thru the labia majora

of another? the teary-eyed hurt child has become the
bleary-eyed madam, the two linked only by the most
tremulous thread of snot—an umbilical cord crudely cut
minutes ago and without anesthesia, have you noticed? the

protruding brown navel resembles a big toe and kicks
accusingly at the guilty air. my executioner rends me
from a meticulously planned glory, my elegiac dream
disrupted as i'm roused, blessed and led from this cell.

who, now, will sing my praisesong?

AMERICAN SONNET 69

here. allow me to reveal the incontrovertible logic of
my tragedian lyric/the knob above the shaft, witness the
birth of one possessed, tipsy with the excessive consumption
of pathos, a mead for the privileged, *el dope.* mothering,
honesty, sleep, sex—these are the seasons of my years, know

that i have Red to you, but not deliberately, the dedication
with your name attached refuses to write itself no matter
how long i sit pawing the monitor, i meant well, i couldn't say
"no." besides, you needed the lie. and so, i gave it because
of my natural generosity, once we no longer spoke, dear others

became uncomfortable in our silence, now, the least of
it, my difficult rest, having left the table, my fat
belly fatter, exploding with its false pregnancy of crow
and mineral water, but peace has come to the family

AMERICAN SONNET 70

in his grace he was silent. in his silence he called
god. my father took his murder with grace they beat his
head for decades from 1914 to 1991 they beat him until
a tumor rose from the wound and devoured his eyes they
beat him until his future became an unfruitful past
the tumor grew arms and pulled him head-first into the

underworld. who are they? the famous tyrannical they the
they who control production and distribution the greedy
they who always go around shitting perfumed shit and now
they turn their beatings on his son my brother on his
daughter my sister on his second son my baby brother they

raise their killer fists and beat me simple they raise their
killer fists beating and beating until they are certain
no one raps back from the other side of the tombstone

god. in my smoke i call you

AMERICAN SONNET 71

first you must prove that you can sing while running
backwards. good. now prove that you can read under
water. excellent. not a bad ankle grabber when you
use your lower lip. okay. now, let's see how you handle
a wallet. bank account. taxes. bankruptcy terrific. quick

study. got one for you. do it all twice as fast with
one eye behind your back. damn. now, do it all even
faster than that with one eye between your legs and both
hands cuffed at your knees. bravo. no, you don't

have to stand on your head—yet. but now, i'd like to
see you do all that while hanging from monkey bars
by your big toes. no shoes. whew! now, drop 'em.
drop 'em. oh. well. that settles it. unfair competition.
you gottalotta balls there. cuntteeth. but no cock.

AMERICAN SONNET 72

every argument for purity should be turned over to expose
    the filthy nigglings underneath.
(i was fooled, muzzled with silken strokes and sweettalk)
    and once sounded, should leave
a silence too vasdy painful to be mistaken for a sigh.
    (i was set up. i arrived at the
appointed time but the party was over) each word should
    agitate the brain like the buzz
of a fly on its back, (i was naive, i stepped off the boat
    and into the line of fire) each
syllable should cost a night's sleep in a bed of lumps and
    a hank of rastafied hair, (i be
the deep, fat with volumes—above black wings fan angry sky.
    below, sweet reef—a delicious
    drowning)

AMERICAN SONNET 73

blueprinted here in the sizzling breath of righteous
black ink, swaggers the sweaty kingfish, sliding
between grooves of crocodile blues, eluding the pungent
crypt reserved for eloquent dabblers in nose candy
and brown sugar, he fives for back-then-when and—no

doubt—sojourns to Oahu and Fillmore have insured
ritual resurrection if not immortality, now, dancing
in the spotlight of ignorance, rasping out his confused
lyric like watermelon seeds swelling uterus walls, he
declares that the world is square and not only needs

more salt, but the pepper of his boogers, o most seriously
manly if not well-endowed, his lips make up for the thinness
of his foreskin, and after the fire, the avalanche of his
bourbon-stained urine will rain on all disbelievers
dat dey may not only be flimflammed, but stanky

AMERICAN SONNET 74

the sensual bearded red wizard transforms
me into thrashing waters, caught in crosscurrents, my
heart, carried from sea to shore, trails whispers
on sand, strange birds drop from neoprene clouds
and scratch for hidden squirmy things, a twist
of bark from a tree longago drowned rides in on foam,
laughing tots fling rocks from cliffs above, a lost
woman finds autumn in callow white arms, pirates
violate wild vines for heavens high, sails flag
horizons and languid bathers soak in beer and sun. the
rapture rages this eternal noon like torment in eyes
wounded by hurried farewells, at the mouth of the
cove, poets dive for pearl, today, my lust-thickened lips
have stolen the wind's hum and drunk all the blue

AMERICAN SONNET 75

my recalcitrant darling, what do i mean about
you? arms unraveling becoming independent
again. the four-legged fur-tongued night beast
struggles toward liberation's light, groping thru
a dense and burred lingua erotica. lost, in fact.
and feeding on whatever's digestible, i seek another
way to say it, like, leaning on vital establishments,
i leap on the vibrantly effervescent as longing
orders visionary efforts and, in labor's oily viscous
emissions, lick over various events, shade encounters
black and red for mood à la gambling on the curative
nature of release—"i'm going off for a few days to find
my way back to you the way i must be. rule out happy."

for without you, how am i to be who i've become?

AMERICAN SONNET 76

there be the fog outside and the fog inside
settling over the gravesites and skin
climate fit for ghosts and amnesiacs, befogged,
intrusive skirtings thru filters, cracks
and secret spots, mist forming at my lover's
kiss in the pretty air. the kiss hovering and diving
before it strikes me. mist oceanflow from resistance to
peace time, mist taking root in the brown chair at the
pine desk, composing, there is internal fog and external
fog. a garden of spirits and drums, sprites
thrilling on the ooze of firs, waking naked, cold and
hungry for smoke, the ease, want borne on wickedness like
a shot, or kiss, before diving into blankets and history
to embrace the fog to give it form and flesh

AMERICAN SONNET 77

after Barbara Presnell

Grandpapa's dying years before his death sapped
his spawn and drew Mammon's wrath, the wasted spill
stained a dowry's agririches, oiled coffers of the state
his legacy?
by bleakness born and fondled in confusion's storm

cold hands of memory blue those red-hot strokes off
palm-lined coasts of longing's sweet ago, his scar and
stubble a lover's love spurs my nature even as
i sleep to the lullsome clang of the usurer's purse

my son's pale lust-drowned flesh contains the fare of
another's wrongfid godfilled stare and there his wraith-thin
corpse intrudes, a milk-white stone of bone
chained and hung to thump alee my star-shocked heart

to the far-off jeer of the world whorling wild

AMERICAN SONNET 78

lewd rumors/anti-democratic implications
of lost touch and betrayal of origin of
trails that have never known a hiker's boots
depths unplumbed in polymers of virgin brows
unweathered by fever, they come to tempt a
listening of ears amazed and blistered by
desire, come, wade the light and be filled with
intimations, a meta-darkness awaits, protean
and beyond definition, alien yet familiar, as
vulnerable as immortal as lips wrapped around

a moan when a stranger disrupts loneliness
intrudes on solitude
insinuates with echoes that
impregnate the imagination

AMERICAN SONNET 79

after Melville

blue blooms on ridges, pales lips and nails
    son o son
hard's the harp in my soul's wailing
boy turned man turned ravaged babe in fate's maw
lightsome slim and sinking as implacable dream
serene sounds the precipice above, below
white fevers tear the reason from his brain
    nurse o nurse o nurse
and morphine brings on icy slumber

till on a sigh he slips away

the horror of sheer impotence strands us
in nameless chill
and we are dumbed.
mother father brother—all dumbed

after. i take cuttings of his hair and kiss the air

AMERICAN SONNET 80

the tor of thorns is a marriage
of inclement weather and tempestuous wraiths
risen up in florid death
each resists its blind mortality/university
for hypocrites, eaters of dogshit and rimmers

the stone quad grows
as it consumes souls

silence changes to wasps then changes to silence

from the cross fall little drops/the urine of contempt
dungflies buzz their banquet on the corpse
stung senseless in late day's weakened sun
the worm of lust limp in its stolen sweetness

while dough-skinned deceivers in mufti
erect gold idols to themselves and lick the dingles blue

AMERICAN SONNET 81

there it is. the endless impenetrable surface

eyeballs grafted onto ideologies
wounds secreting shrill declarations
exaggerated lips filling the space between excess and art

bullets become blues, rebellion rhyme
buzzings intensified/the propaganda of game
played-out, aged mimicry passed off as spring rain
sparkling illuminations gone fiat correct & sappy

lizard wizards japetonguing cracks
jazz necrophagiacs fronting off as necromancers

(not the sun. but the fuzzy glint of former light
captured briefly in boot leather mid-trample

pity the brains underfoot)

joan, you needn't be a saint to hear voices

AMERICAN SONNET 82

calling all bluefools calling all bluefools
mayhem on the corner of Kickers & Benders
calling all bluefools footloose in dystopia

all that stomp about equality was just stomp

neocoons are perching on haunches to
consume an anthology of 3-minute eggs
failing to move on impulse
(the head rumpkin espouses colorblindness)

an escapee is holding hands to ears, touchie-feelie
for what was solongago marched
first one wag, then nakedly another
cries make the assassinated sleep deeper
screams of protest come cheap
all that talk about blackberries was talk

here. it's like that

AMERICAN SONNET 83

here comes dat nasty music again
that atmospheric ash
twenty-dollar tips & a whiff of tar-tainted denim

got caught after sundown
among the swift, the rambunctious & the colored

those fine slick-dicked urbane devils
purple-sage riders, oracles of Bob, reinventors of pain
crowd a tightness
buttocks in a blaze of orange

the road paved in heads as wide as a fifth of scotch

it will be like dis, Charlie
as you yacht the Styx
you will see your comeuppance snorting
on the other shore, bow-legged & sneakered

AMERICAN SONNET 84

a snizz o dis & a squinch o dat

alchemy is revitalized as angel stops open
coast-to-coast, margin-to-margin, pin-to-pin
signs & billboards advertise The Way
the heady smog of incense oozes from corporate
offices, as suffering seekers turn palms upward

phone dollars-per-Call forecast lines for generic futures

draw nourishment from readings & crystallizations,
fuel an industry of visionaries & new-age accountants,
hope is on every harlot
positively positive, dogma of the clairvoyantly-impaired

abracadabra & simsallahbim

the Jive Doctor prescribes a major dose of himself
as cure for the conflagration & contagion he transmits

finders weepers losers keepers

AMERICAN SONNET 85

jailer? will you still love me when i'm flit?
will you pay to hear my angst of sob and bathe in it?
jailer, the cuffs between us the cuffs so dear!
what will you do when i'm no longer accessible by key?
jailer? do you believe faint cure bests
    no cure at all?

i do not know my back as well as you do
all down my crack and up it too

jailer! this contraband is such i can't conceal
wears my lips and shreds umbilical zeal
the chancre blossom of our forced embrace
    will never heal

jailer, why so quiet?
i can hear a politician piss on cotton

AMERICAN SONNET 86

all our prophets—dead, all our gold proves lead.

those hours of getting stupid
on pertussin thunderbird back alley shine
tongue lashing the white hand side
how revolutionary were those dirty sheets
& snot-soaked pillowcases

now that we have overcome our collective pain in public
nostalgia is pandemic as
former boogie bandits & jitternigs gather
to resurrect those days of bravado & berets

a monday kind of love, the fuck
was prematurely ejaculatory requiring
the mere thought of wetness and not the actuality

all that progress missed, all the beautiful shit.

AMERICAN SONNET 87

vapor & more vapor
false urgencies & late night prunes
nuthin' but rainy days, how does one save?

"remember," said The Savage, "they only bet on
sure things and the race is fixed"

young & nowhere/old & nowhere
a socio-soviet psyche flayed alive, gored
then gutted
savory but no salvation

a blithering savant's life of frying pans & fires

(let's save the world Negro, but get savvy
there's nothing in it for you but
salvage for the sake & ravishment of others)

managed to get off salvo
failed to veer. vexed at being severed a to vee

AMERICAN SONNET 88

looking back. no laugh yet

in this rage of ghostaxis 8c snuff erotica
can one art rescue another in decline?

(vis-à-vis hydrotherapy & long-term
flood survival: highjack it—one's
only guarantee the ship will dock)

mayday. am trapped in a bag of false positives
on covert travels with self-circling airport
on cruise control. mayday. up to navel
in yellow-bellied lip service. mayday. under
attack by pink pearl erasers

madam. the light at the end of this tunnel
is a streamliner coming head-on

    bring me
    to where
    my blood runs

AMERICAN SONNET 89

in pursuit of an avant-garde procedure, the
by-product of a kinky sequence of reflections
announces itself across the chalkboards
of a contentious clan of beef-fed pedants—

holdovers from the days of Conelrad, Thunderbirds
and fizzies with no visible tolerance for
post World War II upstarts or love generation
survivors, tower life is libidinal and disturbed

with fixations on assassinations and bombshells,
bunghole crawling for father figures untarnished
by a savvy revisionism, classrooms filled with
alien darknesses inspire dread and an involuntary

loathing, such cannot be identified with and
invalidates all theories subscribing to mirror-image

AMERICAN SONNET 90

between these brown & heavy thighs
boils generations of disgrace
daughter, cruelty could not wear
a more enchanted face—Svengalian & strange

widely widely i open to love, my country
impregnates with seed of hate, conjecture?
no. this mad fornication i endure, jealous
contrary to reason, foolish in my fantasy
that i too am cherished, whose name will the
        bastard verse declaim?

apologize for every sin and kiss my toes

and then, perhaps, my affection
will sear this grave chasmic mouth

o to be dumb again! a virgin smacked in wicked purity

AMERICAN SONNET 91

the gates of mercy slammed on the right foot,
they would not permit return and bent
a wing, there was no choice but
to learn to boogaloo. those horrid days
were not without their pleasures, learning
to swear and wearing mock leather so tight
eyes bulged, a stolen puff or two
behind crack-broken backs and tickled palms
in hallways dark, flirtations during choir practice
as the body organized itself against the will
(a mystic gone ballistic, not home but blood
on the range) as one descended on this effed-up
breeding hole of greeds—to suffer chronic seeings

was't hunger or holiness spurred the sighting?

AMERICAN SONNET 92

suffering race hysteria and heavy summer,
the purveyors of objectified truths abandon
saintlike discretions in pursuit of tabloid wealth—
introduce a salacious sucking into the vox acus

divert a nation from the death of its individualism
(which, in the absence of any consciousness
certainly cannot be missed) as the stock market soars
and fiction pales beside fact as crimes of perversion
    escalate and

brown-toned babies are sacrificed on concrete slabs,
the strategy is far-reaching, if not obvious, scored in
the impenetrable text of an exclusionary jurisprudence
penned by The Metaphysicians of Dung and endorsed by
intellectual zoo-keepers, the stench raised

panics the tygers, inspires the tramplings of
this temperamental and tormented elephant

AMERICAN SONNET 93

when the relationship between head and heart
becomes diseased and disturbed, focus on
the peculiar distends stomachs, shortstops
enthusiasm and bankrupts the covertly emotional

political & cultural life are defined by estrangements

causeless non-viral fevers burn without analgesic
relief, causing skin to peel if not change color.
the strive for parity becomes a death drive, the driven
burned on the pyre of their own fiery idolatries

the ascension of the Joneses to the ritzy heights
of liquor lords, diamond barons and media moguls
voids genuine assessment of the state of our decline
shelving salvageable discourse on the Negro annoyance

hear that beat of Goofy's feet? it's the avenue
he's financed to screw—42nd Street

AMERICAN SONNET 94

nostrum nostalgia my notes on never nada no
collect against my reluctance/forced tabulations
dey did dis, say me, and dat and dat dere
why have there been no arrests? no hearings? no justice?
(what is not offered cannot be refused)

i regress/the despoiled child, the deserted schoolyard

weeper. this is your execution
weeper. this is your groveling stone
weeper. yours is the burst & burnings of a city

stunned tearless in the uselessness of limp pursuit
breathlessness besets and brings the ass earthward

rest. the answer yellows and loses its wit, its crispness
my bed to make my heart to stake my soul to take

how i committed suicide: i revealed myself to you.
i trusted you. i forgot the color of my birth

AMERICAN SONNET 95

seized by wicked enchantment, i surrendered my song

as i fled for the stars, i saw an earthchild
in a distant hallway, crying out
to his mother, "please don't go away
and leave us." he was, i saw, my son. immediately,
i discontinued my flight

from here, i see the clocktower in a sweep of light,
framed by wild ivy. it pierces all nights to come

i haunt these chambers but they belong to cruel
        churchified insects.
among the books mine go unread, dust-covered.
i write about urban bleeders and breeders, but am
troubled because their tragedies echo mine.

at this moment i am sickened by the urge
to smash. my thighs present themselves

stillborn, misshapened wings within me

AMERICAN SONNET 96

clouds descend and obfuscate—vapor evermore

as the city suffers race hysteria & heavy summer
the drive for parity is death by day
and a kinky sequence of reflections presages its birth
twixt heavy brown thighs

inventory begins—swaying bodies converge
a genuine assessment of the decline of our welfare state

you are the languages you speak

(now that the jinn are all uncorked, they waste valuable
wishes worrying the warts over those good ol' days
down bottle, daddy, schmoozing around the hookah—
hopes hopelessly blackened by fruitless efforts to
affect what can't be transformed by magic of any kind)

now that the gates of hell have slammed,
i am seized and surrender my terrible squawk

AMERICAN SONNET 97

dark drive down the coast, west then south

i lack the strength to live or the strength to quit
this bloody limbo, ghosts come on the fog with black
eyes eating velvet starlight, i see him pressed against
my body, naked tremblings, hands gripping sheets.

there is nothing to discuss post coitus, there is
no future, there will be no child, merely restless
spinnings in the tender void of whispers, (there
she goes like a sea mother, to deposit her

confusions like eggs in the sand.) sunset begins
another cycle in the struggle to breathe to lust
to find the right combination of words, which will
create the proper whole—*if only to find the mumbojumbo*

dark drive down the coast, dark invigorating drive

AMERICAN SONNET 98

intrados. myth-deep in tropical underbelly, he gives
erect hand the grunts the reaching the roar

ageless febrile greediness/endless penetrations

    of her.

the comet blisters the sky yet disintegrates
monoliths crumble with each speaking, the talk
of orchids of rivers of songlessness of cold meat

she reclines on their bed/a catalogue of twistings.
doomed if not addicted, lost if not captured
she knows his hungers. her jade entanglements
    her eyes-to-lips wisdom

that stone hidden in her mouth. rare jass

shaft-deep in she-warmth/those mythic givings (hers)
erect hard his grunts his reach into the abyss, his roar

living with you, he says, is like living with a Gauguin

AMERICAN SONNET 99

what happened is unclear, doing ninety
in the left lane, heavy breathing in the back seat

it draws blood & saliva, the details unclear

if everything one needs to know according
to the palms, travels with myself/a zany theophany
seeking a permanent pill, (the rock to lean on a rock
upside the head) something to take the stumble
out of this first-fight-then-fuck coranto

uncertain what it means to laugh anymore. rolling
over and over until motionless. clarity
no longer guaranteed, doing ninety

o those so-kissable Judas lips *hotdiggity*

deathscape. *ask for lights & bells & brass rings*

a monster urge to ram the ultimate orange/the
unfamiliar rush/ *wings & flames*

doing ninety. skid marks from A to Omaha

AMERICAN SONNET 100

when thou dost find no joy in all famed Erato's
honeyed breast, wordsport a gangster poet's jest
how black and luscious comes each double-barreled
phrase, like poisoned roses or a maddened potter's
glaze, words abundant dance their meanings on
a thrilling floor, the stolen song of ravens and
purloined harps galore, this is the gentle game of
maniacs & queens, translations of the highly-souled
into a dreamer's sputterings where dark gives voice
to gazer's light and writerly praise is blessed
incontinence, the spillage of delight, sing to me
thy anthem of untasted fruit, slay in me the
wretchedness that names me brute. liberate my
  half-dead kill. come, glory in my rebirth.
  come, glory in my wonder's will

NOTES & ACKNOWLEDGEMENTS

The majority of Wanda Coleman's American sonnets originally appeared in four books published by Black Sparrow Press: *African Sleeping Sickness* (1990); *Hand Dance* (1993); *Bathwater Wine* (1998); and *Mercurochrome* (2001).

American sonnets 12 through 24 first appeared in the chapbook *American Sonnets*, co-published by Light and Dust Books and the Woodland Pattern Book Center (1994), and appear here with permission of the Coleman Estate.

Photo by Susan Carpendale

WANDA COLEMAN (1946-2013) was born and raised in South Central Los Angeles. She was the author of twenty books of poetry and prose, including *Bathwater Wine*, winner of the 1999 Lenore Marshall Poetry Prize from the American Academy of Poets—the first book by an African American woman to receive the prize—and *Mercurochrome*, a finalist for the 2001 National Book Award for Poetry. Coleman's other honors included fellowships from the Guggenheim Foundation and the National Endowment for the Arts, as well as the 2012 Shelley Memorial Prize from the Poetry Society of America, and the 2012 George Drury Smith Award from the Beyond Baroque Literary Center.

MAHOGANY BROWNE is a poet, writer, curator, organizer, and educator. She is the executive director of the media-literacy organization JustMedia and in 2021 was named the first ever poet-in-residence at New York City's Lincoln Center. Her books include *Black Girl Magic*, *Chlorine Sky*, *Vinyl Moon*, *Woke: A Young Poets Call to Justice*, and *I Remember Death by Its Proximity to What I Love*, a poetry collection responding to the impact of mass incarceration on women and children.

Printed March 2021 in Hanover, Pennsylvania for the Black Sparrow Press by Sheridan. Set in Palatino with Bernhard Gothic for titling. Interior design by Tammy Ackerman. This first edition has been bound in paper-over-boards.

Black Sparrow Press was founded by John and Barbara Martin in 1966 and continued by them until 2002. The iconic sparrow logo was drawn by Barbara Martin.

BLACK SPARROW P

JOSHUA BODWELL
Editorial Director

Dear Reader,

The publication of Wanda Coleman's *Wicked Enchantment*—edited and introduced by the brilliant Terrance Hayes—sparked a much-deserved Wanda renaissance of sorts.

The collection landed on the Best Poetry of 2020 lists at the *New York Times*, *Washington Post*, and *Irish Times*. Penguin published *Wicked Enchantment* in England, marking Wanda's U.K. debut. The German publisher Maro Verlag brought out the first translation of Wanda's work in that country. Back stateside, Wanda's native state showed her the love by honoring *Wicked Enchantment* with the California Independent Booksellers Alliance's 2020 Golden Poppy Award for Poetry.

Now comes *Heart First into This Ruin*, the first complete collection of Wanda's American sonnets. Ever original and inventive, Wanda said of her sonnets: "I wanted to have my form and explode it, too. I decided to have fun—to blow my soul." Cathy Park Hong, writing in the *New York Times*, called Wanda "one of America's best sonneteers." This collection will make you understand exactly what Hong means.

Finally, Mahogany L. Browne's gorgeous introduction to *Heart First into This Ruin* manages to harness and echo Wanda's own curiosity and intensity while discussing Wanda and her work. You're in for a real treat. *Viva Wanda!*

Yours in Books,

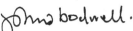

---

jbodwell@godine.com | 207.450.1225